Potatoes

by Ann L. Burckhardt

Reading Consultant:
Chuck Kostichka

Bridgestone Books
an Imprint of Capstone Press

Bridgestone Books are published by Capstone Press
818 North Willow Street, Mankato, Minnesota 56001
Copyright © 1996 by Capstone Press

Library of Congress Cataloging-in-Publication Data
Burckhardt, Ann, 1933-
    Potatoes/ by Ann L. Burckhardt
    p. cm.--(Early-reader science. Foods.)
    Includes bibliographical references (p. 24) and index.
    Summary: Simple text introduces potatoes, and instructions are given for making a
    potato stamper.
    ISBN 1-56065-451-1
    1.Potatoes--Juvenile literature. 2. Nature craft--Juvenile literature. [1. Potatoes.]
    I. Title. II. Series.
SB211.P8B878 1996
641.3'521--dc20

                                                96-26569
                                                 CIP
                                                  AC

Photo credits
Unicorn/James A. Hayes, cover; Paul A. Hein, 12; Bob Garas, 16.
FPG International, 4, 8, 14, 18, 20.
Chuck Place, 6.
International Stock, 10.

Table of Contents

Words in **boldface** type in the text are defined in the Words to Know section in the back of this book.

What Are Potatoes?

Potatoes are one of the most important crops in the world. They are sometimes called spuds. The average person in North America eats more than 100 pounds (45 kilograms) of potatoes every year.

Different Kinds of Potatoes

There are more than 5,000 kinds of potatoes. The most common are red, russet, and white.

Parts of a Potato

A potato has brown, white, or red skin. The skin has small dents called eyes. Under the skin is the **flesh**.

Where Potatoes Grow

Potatoes can grow almost anywhere. They can grow in the desert or on a mountain. Russia grows the most potatoes. In North America, Idaho grows the most potatoes.

How Potatoes Grow

A chunk of potato can be planted to grow more potatoes. The chunk must have a sprouting eye. Potatoes grow under the ground. The leaves, flowers, and fruits of the potato plant grow above the ground.

Harvest

When the tops of the potato plant die, the potatoes are ready to **harvest**. The potatoes are dug up from the ground. They are washed to remove the soil.

How We Use Potatoes

Potato chips and French fries come from potatoes. Potatoes are also served mashed or baked. Instant potato flakes are sometimes used for snow in the movies.

History

The Irish people used to depend on potatoes to survive. In 1845, a **fungus** killed Ireland's potato crop. The people began to starve. One million people died and 1.5 million **emigrated**.

Potatoes and People

Mr. Potato Head is a popular toy. It was once made from a real potato. Today, it is made from plastic. A person who watches TV a lot and never exercises is sometimes called a couch potato.

Hands On: Make Potato Stampers

You can make cards, wrapping paper, or pictures with a potato stamper. You can make your own designs and use your own colors. Your potato stampers will not be like anyone else's.

You will need
- potatoes
- a pen
- paper
- a knife
- paints

1. Cut a potato in half.
2. Use a pen to draw a simple design or shape on the flesh side of each potato half.
3. Cut around your design with a knife. Cut about 1/2 inch (1.25 centimeters) deep.
4. Cut away the part of the potato outside the design. Your design should stand out from the rest of the potato.
5. Dip your potato design in paint and stamp it on paper.
6. Rinse the paint off your potato if you want to try a different color.
7. Make as many different designs as you like. You can use the stamps over and over.

Words to Know

emigrate—leave your native country to settle in another

flesh—the edible part of a fruit or vegetable

fungus—a fast-growing plant that feeds off another plant

harvest—gather a crop

Read More

Hughes, Meredith Sayles and E. Thomas Hughes. *The Great Potato Book*. New York: MacMillan, 1986.

Selsam, Millicent. *More Potatoes!* New York: Harper & Row, 1972.

Turner, Dorothy. *Potatoes*. Minneapolis: Carolrhoda, 1989.

Watts, Barrie. *Potato*. Morristown, N.J.: Silver Burdett Press, 1988.

Index